Protest

Hannah Lavery

T0284348

methuen | drama

LONDON • NEW YORK • OXFORD • NEW DELHI • SYDNEY

METHUEN DRAMA
Bloomsbury Publishing Plc
50 Bedford Square, London, WC1B 3DP, UK
1385 Broadway, New York, NY 10018, USA
29 Earlsfort Terrace, Dublin 2, Ireland

BLOOMSBURY, METHUEN DRAMA and the Methuen
Drama logo are trademarks of Bloomsbury Publishing Plc

First published in Great Britain 2023

Series design by Rebecca Heselton

Cover image © photka/Shutterstock

A catalogue record for this book is available from the British Library.

A catalog record for this book is available from the Library of Congress.

ISBN: PB: 978-1-3504-2814-0
ePDF: 978-1-3504-2815-7
eBook: 978-1-3504-2816-4

Series: Plays for Young People

Typeset by Mark Heslington Ltd, Scarborough, North Yorkshire

To find out more about our authors and books visit
www.bloomsbury.com and sign up for our newsletters.

Protest was originally co-commissioned and co-produced by Fuel, Imaginate and Northern Stage in association with National Theatre of Scotland. It was developed and supported by the Scottish Government's Festivals Expo Fund and Imaginate's Accelerator programme. Accelerator is supported by the PLACE programme, funded by the Scottish Government (through Creative Scotland), the City of Edinburgh Council and the Edinburgh Festivals. Supported by the Binks Trust.

Protest was part of the Edinburgh International Children's Festival and toured throughout Scotland in May–June 2023. Its first performance was on 26 April 2023 at Northern Stage in Newcastle-upon-Tyne with the following cast and creative team:

Alice	**Kirsty Maclaren**
Jade	**Tamara Fairbairn**
Chloe	**Esmé Kingdom**
Writer	Hannah Lavery
Director	Natalie Ibu
Associate Director	Natasha Haws
Set and Costume Designer	Amy Jane Cook
Sound Design	Novasound
Movement Director	Nadia Iftkhar

Protest

Characters

Alice, *east coast Scottish*
Jade, *east coast Scottish, mixed heritage (Jamaican and Scottish)*
Chloe, *English (Northumberland), mixed heritage (Scottish and Irish)*

Act One

Three Girls

Scene One: Here Is a Girl

Three girls stand. There are sounds of a forest. The sound of a road. The sounds of a school playground. The sound of a school bell . . .

Alice   Here is a girl.

Jade   Here is a girl.

Chloe   Here is a girl.

Alice   Sitting at the kitchen table.

Jade   Running home.

Chloe   Kicking leaves in the woods.

Something changes.

Jade   My friend is crying . . . My best friend is crying . . . I want my mum . . . She will know what to do . . . There must be something that can be done.

Chloe   I am wondering if I have time to climb that tree. If I can avoid scuffing my new shoes. I open my rucksack, take out a plastic bag, start collecting the rubbish left on the ground. I will be late home again.

Alice   My mum is on the phone. My dad is making dinner. I am waiting . . . Waiting to say something.

Something I have been thinking about all week. All week . . . Seven whole days.

Scene Two: Run

Alice   Mum says I ran before I walked. That I would drive her demented running up and down the flat . . . I remember being wee and running full pelt across the beach . . . Trying to chase the gulls . . . Arms out like another bird.

My gran was a runner at school, long distance. So not a sprinter like me and Mum but she taught me how to use my arms to sort of propel myself forward. So not like wings but like . . . Grabbing at the air! . . .

Ack! It's hard to explain.

Gran says it's in my genes – the running. That some are just born runners. We are born runners. Born to run! . . . Mum takes me with her when she goes running. I have to turn back after a mile or so but my mum she just goes on and on . . . I like to watch her as she heads over the hill at the end of the estate. My dad says she is a superwoman. I think she is more like the wind or something – like the weather. A force of nature . . . Unstoppable . . . Un-catchable.

She stops, remembering her mother. She sees her running away from her.

Hailey, my best friend, is fast too. Not as fast as me but still really fast. We race each other at break. The boys take up most of the playground playing football, but we have found this strip at the edge of the grass that we can run up and down on practising our sprinting. At lunchtime we do circuits of the playground, trying to avoid the games of football. We're in training. You see, at the end of the year, at the end of sports day, there is the big relay race. All the P7 classes put forward a team. A team of four runners, the fastest and best runners are always the first runner and the last runner. The last runner – the anchor.

There are three P7 classes so that's three teams. It's a big deal. The last big thing of primary school. I have been dreaming about being the last runner – about being the anchor for our class since P1.

But, and here is the issue . . . My problem – right?

See, everybody says boys are faster – even though me and Hailey are the fastest. Even though we are the actual fastest. It is always Rory and Josh. Rory and Josh. Rory and Josh – always. I mean I can beat anyone in the year – anyone. Even in my normal school shoes with their slippy soles and you know Rory and Josh have their grippy leather shoes, but still even in my school skirt and tights – I am the fastest. I am the best runner in the whole year.

But you know?

Miss Thomas will choose Rory and Josh as the first and last. Rory will be the anchor. Even though we would win. Me and Hailey would absolutely win it for the class. Mum says I should make the boys give up some more of the space in the playground. Boys always take up all the space, she says, then Dad told Mum that things are different now. I was confused, I suppose like – what is different now? And also, what was different then? I mean I did suffragettes at school but that was long before even Gran . . . See? Mum says I can do anything I want to do – but is that true?

Like if all the space, like in the playground, is taken up by the boys?

Like in class the boys are always more . . . Like, needing more – right?

Like, they talk louder and get more attention.

Like even the books Miss Thomas choses for us are all geared to the boys – to get them interested – right?

Like I'm not saying I don't like stories about boys but – you know?

I would quite like the next class novel to have a girl as the hero – the main character – right?

You know what I mean?

Like even Hermione is not the main character – is she?

6 Protest

Hailey's birthday is two weeks after mine and since nursery we have always had a joint party. Our mums are pals so it makes sense . . . We usually want the same thing, like a theme. This year we thought we'd have this sports day theme because – you know? It's us.

Hailey has a really big garden and so we thought we'd like to set up different activities to complete and then we would have a sort of Olympic ceremony.

Hailey's mum put together a prize winners podium out of a nest of tables. We had chocolate medals in the party bags. The thing is two of the girls, Lucy and Poppy, had on these party dresses and they were so afraid they would get into trouble if they messed them up or ruined their shoes, they just sat it out. Like the whole thing! Even the things they could have done. I mean what's the point of party dresses – like how much fun can you really have when you are frightened of your own clothes – right?

'Mum?'

I have to say her name three times before she puts down her phone. Dad has to call her too. Alice is talking to you, he says. Not angry. We all know how hard she has to work. She is not afraid of hard work, she says. I am not sure she is afraid of anything.

'Mum?'

'Sorry sweetheart', she says.

'I am the fastest in class', I tell her.

Then it all comes out. Miss says she is going to make it a vote – a vote!

After telling us all year how fast Rory and Josh are, Miss says to make it fair we will have a vote for each place in the relay. I mean, that's not right – is it? Obviously everyone will just vote for the boys.

Rory will be the anchor. Then, I start to cry . . . 'How do you know?' she says. 'Know what?' I say

'Know that you are faster?' she says.

'Of course, we are faster! I know them, I have watched them running for the whole of primary, I know I can beat them. We can beat then . . . Easy. We can beat them, Mum. We can. I can beat them.'

'Okay, Alice, prove it', she says.

'What?'

'Prove it . . . To them. To all of them', she says.

'What do you mean?'

'Race them, love. Challenge them to a race. They won't give anything up unless you fight for it', she says . . .

'Is this really about Alice?' my dad whispers to her.

But of course it is . . . Why wouldn't it be? . . . And I think, I think my mum is a genius. A genius. 'I will race them. So they can't deny it. They will have to vote for us then.' Mum does a 'Whoop!' at that. 'That's my girl', she says. And Dad says, 'Well, if anyone can change the world, you two can'. Yes, we can, I shout. 'And you will', mum winks.

Jade I grab her hand and we run. Flat out. Running. Their words, flying at us. 'Sticks and stones may break my bones but words will never hurt me' . . . But she is crying now. I am crying now too. They hurt.

The words. Those words hurt me. We explode into the house.

My mum comes running down the stairs. I am crying really hard now.

It takes a while before I can speak and for Leila even longer.

Mum is so angry.

I hear her voice cracking . . . Breaking . . . Broken voice on the phone to the school . . . I watch her after she's put the phone down . . . Just sitting on the sofa, rubbing her hands together and staring like she does when she's trying not to cry . . . Like she did after Granda.

When Leila's mum comes for Leila, they talk for a long time in our front room . . .

Leila and I have been best friends since nursery. We are the only brown girls in our class. Leila red brown, deep brown, strong shining brown, but I am brown like a pebble on the floor of a burn. In the summer, I am silt. In the winter, sand. Nana says my skin is like sun dapples. I am not sure what dapples means, but it is nice that word . . . Dapples.

Leila is the cleverest girl in our class, the whole year probably, but I'm a bit better at maths and art. She talks all the time . . . Good talking . . . I like to listen. I am a good listener. Good talker, good listener . . . A perfect match. Two peas in a pod.

Kindred spirits. Sister friends . . .

Leila and I cycle to school together every day. Leila's bike is white and gold.

My bike is red and black. That day . . .

We left our bikes.

Ran home through the woods.

Our dads had to go and get them later. My bike was missing its seat.

Leila's had lost its gold ribbons.

Chloe *starts to climb.*

Chloe   Our house is beside the woods. There is not so much countryside left in our town, lots of new houses were built on the fields, and the woods used to be a lot bigger, but they say the bit between the estate and the school is protected.

I hope that's true.

There is this really special place in the woods where the deer come, and if you sit really quietly they will ignore you and you can watch them, draw them.

Teenagers have started coming to the woods at night, it is full now of broken bottles and all sorts of rubbish. I try to pick it all up. I've even got a special litter picker from the internet for the glass and other things I don't want to touch.

I go out most mornings and in the afternoons after school.

There is always loads of crisp packets blown over from the playground and takeaway boxes and wrappers too, I think people throw them out their car windows, and it makes its way down here –

Jade   – My dad has lived all his life here, in our wee town. He's friends with everyone.

It takes us ages to walk down the high street, cause he's always stopping to say hello – to Jean and her dog, to the guys at Home Hardware, to Marty at the record store, to Billy and Tam, to Jenny, to Rory at the bakery, to Jo at Crunchy Carrot to . . . to everybody and to anybody. Mum says, he has time for the whole town but no time left for himself but he can't help it, he's just like that wi' folk – you know? Always asking after them, making a joke, and if they need it – helping out . . . He's in the lifeboat crew too like Granda was, and Granda's dad was and Granda's dad's dad was . . . He's one of life's helper-outers, Nan says. A helper-outer – I like that.

And even if he starts talking to someone about something sad, by the end of their chat they'll be laughing . . . like when Jean's dog was ill, they sat together for a long time at the bench at the top of the high street, he gave her his handkerchief and I think some money, but I don't know if he did for sure or what he really said, cause he'd asked me to go get some milk, but I didn't, I just stood outside the shop, and watched him with Jean . . . And after she had a wee cry, Dad said something to her, and she just broke into this big smile, started laughing. They both did . . .

It was like magic . . . His magic . . . He's magic. Dad says, 'This is the best town in the world.'

'The best wee place in the whole wide world', he says. And I believe him . . .

Or I did believe him, I suppose –

Chloe   – I worry about the deer. I worry about them standing on the glass, or the birds, I worry about them getting trapped in the plastic . . . It makes me chest sore –

Alice   – So on Monday before the vote, we race the boys, in front of the whole class at break. We win. Easily.

Okay, not that easy, but we definitely win. Hailey and I bounce down the corridors –

Jade   – Leila just wants to play *Minecraft* after, so I let her play. We don't talk about it. At least not then. Dad tells me later, 'This is because of the shock of it all.'

Mum comes to talk to me at bedtime that night. I tell her again about what happened. The boys, the words, the way we ran. The way they ran after us . . . 'I was scared', I told her. Mum shakes her head and I see the hurt starting in her eyes –

Alice   – The vote happens Tuesday morning, and the class votes for Rory and Josh . . .

Hailey and I will be in the team, but the boys win the vote.

It will be them or rather Rory that will get the finish and the praise, no matter how fast we are, how hard we work to get them in the lead position. It will be Rory that will get to the finish line – I know it sounds like I am just being silly or something and the relay is, as Dad keeps telling me, a team sport but I know, Hailey knows – the whole class saw it.

Maybe we were a bit too full of ourselves – you know? . . . Put people off.

But we are the fastest. I am the fastest. We deserve those spots. I deserve it! We showed them. We proved it – to the whole class. We are the fastest . . .

'If we were boys', Hailey whispers to me. Tears in her eyes –

Chloe   – Before my dad left, he made me this hide in our garden so I could watch the birds –

Jade   – My dad tells me that I should ignore racist people, like those boys, and that 'words won't break my bones' but I suppose . . . I suppose, I feel a bit broken. I feel a bit broken. Not like smashed or that . . . Just knocked a bit, like something has been knocked off me . . . Like when Mum's car got damaged in the Asda car park . . . So? . . . Dented. I feel a bit dented . . . And as much as I try not to be, as much as I try to give Dad my smile . . . I can't. And the thing is neither can he . . . Not one of his real smiles . . . His smile is a bit dented too, I think . . . And he could always find his smile even after Granda – it's his magic . . . So I think, really he's been more dented by what happened than me and I am . . . I am . . . I don't know what I am –

Chloe   – I don't know if he made it knowing he was leaving us, but it's where I go when his not being here gets too much for me –

Alice   – I try to smile back at Hailey to let her know it's no big deal but I am furious. No, I don't think I am angry. Another feeling . . . I am not sure what it is.

Act Two

Good People

Jade My nan is the best nan. I am sorry if that offends you but I can't lie . . . My nan is like sunshine, and rainbows and chocolate biscuits and puppies! She gives the greatest hugs. Tells the best stories. Makes the best ginger cake.

Alice Every Wednesday and Tuesday I go to my gran's after school but even so, it's like my turning up is always a surprise to her. 'Oh, it's you', she will say, as I let myself in. Handing me a hot juice, and going back to her book on the sofa. We snuggle up on cold days and potter in the garden when it's not too bad out. I am a champion weeder. I am always the champion at my gran's. The champion dishwasher. The champion hooverer.

'What's wrong?' she asks that Tuesday afternoon.

'What's wrong with you?'

And I tell her. She takes a long look at me when I have worn myself out.

Jade My nan used to be a nurse, that's where she met Granda. Granda was a fisherman and after he got caught up in his nets, Nan stitched him up in casualty. Granda says by the time she finished sewing him up, he was undone. He loved her the moment he saw her, he said. Nan says that was just the pain relief, the 'gas and air talking'. They were always kidding each other on like that. It was the greatest love story, that's what Mum said at Granda's funeral. Dad started crying when she said that, but Nan told her that was a beautiful thing to say. Sometimes words make you sad for good reasons . . . I loved my granda but Nan loved him more.

Alice 'So, what do you do now?' Gran asks.

'I don't know', I tell her. I don't know.

'Did you think it would be easy?' she asks.

'What?' I say.

'Did you think you would beat the boys and all would be fixed?'

'Yes', I say.

'Of course, you did. You are a champion optimist . . . Just like your mum', she says, pulling me in for a hug.

Jade   Nan says she sometimes forgets he's gone. She says she is always talking to him. When we went round for our dinner that first Sunday after the funeral, she had set a place for him. Dad cried and then Nan cried and then we all cried, but even though it makes us sad, we always set him a place for Sunday dinner now, it's our way of remembering him.

Alice   – My gran said, what Hailey and I did, in racing the boys, was making a stand. Later, I tell Hailey . . . She does one of her big thumbs up at that.

'So what now?' Gran asks.

'Did I not already make my stand?' I say back.

'Well, more like the start of one, now you need to keep going', she says, looking at me like she's going to race me . . . Like she is going to race me and win.

Act Three

School Days

Scene One: Hide

Chloe Dad knew all the names of the birds and knew them just by their calls. He gave me a book about birds for my birthday. I am not as good as him but I am getting there.

We get a lot of birds in our garden. Chaffinches, blue tits, starlings, house sparrows, pigeons, but my favourite is the robin. I think it's because he is always on his own – you never see two robins – do you?

My robin comes right up to the hide, wanting to make friends. 'Good morning', he tweets. 'Good morning, Mr Robin' . . . I like to draw him. I draw him in a wee baseball cap with a rucksack. At bird school. In his nest watching bird tv.

I want to be an illustrator and make children's books about animals when I grow up, just like Beatrix Potter. I've made a whole book already, about Mr Robin. It is quite a sad book though . . . But then he meets a girl who is alone too, and they make friends.

I am not very good with people. I am more of a bird person.

Jade Two weeks after the thing with the boys happened to me and Leila. My dad came home really angry. Dad works in Edinburgh, does things with computers. He gets the train every day, gets home just in time for tea, but this night he was late back. And when he came in, he looked so different. I can't explain. Mum rushed out of the lounge and took him to the kitchen. I listened at the closed door, heard him say to Mum that it made him want to throw up . . . The words, he said, over and over.

The kids will see them.

'Our kids will see them', he said.

'It's on their way to school', he said . . .

He went out with Kenny and Mikey later, came home covered in white paint.

Leila told me after, that she heard her mum say that someone had written some racist words on the big bridge, and drawn swastikas on the school wall.

Next day, all I saw was big sploshes of white paint . . . Like clouds . . . Like beautiful clouds.

We are doing this project on the Second World War, so I know all about swastikas.

I mean, we are so proud that we defeated the Nazis – aren't we?

Chloe   – Beatrix Potter didn't just make books, she also saved a big part of the countryside, she was a conservationist . . .

Jade   I talk to Nan, and she tells me that racists like to use that sign sometimes, the swastika, to scare people, and then she takes this long pause and a big breath and says that folk blame people that are different from them for all the things that are wrong in their lives, and sometimes folk like politicians help them to do that . . .

'Stir hate up, use it like cover, or maybe like a cover? Or a blindfold? To keep us from seeing the folk who are really making our lives hard' . . .

I nod, but I don't really understand . . . Or maybe only the edges of it . . . If that makes sense. Only the edges of it I understand . . .

Our MP came to school to give us a talk . . . It was really boring . . . It got to the point that those with wobbly teeth started to pull . . . Nan thinks this is really funny when I tell her . . . But then she says the are much worse things a

politician can be than boring . . . I nod again, but I don't
understand . . . I don't want boring, I want –

*She whoops and claps like she has just heard the most inspiring and
rousing speech.*

– I want that – you know? Someone that would . . . That
would stop us pulling out our own teeth – right?

Chloe I think I would like to be a conservationist . . . I am
really good at making things safer for the animals in the
wood . . . But I worry . . . I worry that when I'm away on my
holiday to Belfast . . . I don't know how bad it will get . . .
There will be nobody here . . . Nobody.

Jade Nan tells me then about her mum, my great-nana,
about how she came from Jamaica to fight the Nazis, she
served in the RAF – the WAAF, they called it.

After the war, she returned – they were told they were
needed to rebuild the country, but not exactly like a builder
. . . 'We needed help to make us feel normal again', Nan says
. . . And my great nana wanted to help. She was just like my
dad or is he just like her? She helped by working in the
hospital kitchens. She was a cook. I bet she made ginger cake
– I think to ask, but then Nan tells me that her mum said it
was hard for her, that she had thought she would be
welcomed here, but that she found it a cold welcome – that's
what she had said. She had said it was a brittle welcome . . .
One that could snap, break against you. It was only falling in
love with a sweet man (my great-granda) that she got what
she'd been missing – that warmth . . . I said she was starting
to sound like a poem. Nan liked that – 'like a poem', she
repeated – and then she took me to her photo wall to look at
her mum, my great-nana . . . She is beautiful. 'She has
twinkly eyes' – I say.

Her eyes are like Dad's eyes when he laughs, maybe she
laughed like him too or maybe he laughs just like she did . . .
And Nan squeezes my hand, just like she squeezed my hand
at Granda's funeral.

'You know?' she says after a bit of standing quietly.

'There are always good people. There is always kindness, if you look for it.'

I thought about Kenny and Mikey helping Dad paint over the horrible words . . . That was kindness.

I tell Nan, and she says we need another slice of ginger cake. 'How kind', I say in this posh voice as she hands it over, and she laughs and laughs at that . . .

She laughs just like Dad.

Chloe   Last week, someone dumped a mattress in the woods, a great big mattress . . . Covered up a whole patch of snowdrops I was drawing . . . Mum called the council . . . Not about the snowdrops . . . About the mattress.

Jade   I can't say why I started making these posters but maybe it was the conversation with Nan, the one about good people and kindness.

I was drawing a lot in my room after what happened, I was making this picture of our town, the harbour, the fishing boats and then in big dark blue writing, at the top of my picture, I wrote 'BE KIND'.

Chloe   I want to be like Beatrix Potter . . . I do . . . But there is so much to save . . . It's too much for one person, I think . . . Mum says it's too much to worry about. Too much for me to worry about . . .

Jade   It sat on my desk for days. Then one day I put it in my bedroom window . . . Facing out.

Chloe   My brother, he is thirteen, he can be really angry sometimes. Mum says it is not really anger but sadness and also thirteen is a difficult age.

Liam, my brother, used to be really fun, and we would spend ages playing together but he's a teenager now, so he likes to be left alone and play on his phone . . .

Sometimes, when he has been very sad and his sadness has made him slam doors and shout at Mum and storm up to his room, I push a drawing of a laughing seagull called Henry under his door.

Sometimes he says 'Thanks Chloe'. Then I hear him laughing like the seagull, but sometimes he shouts 'Go away!' And sometimes he says nothing, because he is crying so loud . . . And I don't know what to do then . . .

Jade   My window looks out on to the street, and it is a busy street, the main walk to town from our estate. It was there for a few days, maybe less, and then one day, I see that Mrs Cunningham across the road has made a 'Be Kind' poster for her window.

Then Clara at the bottom of the street makes one. Leila makes one too and her neighbours join in.

Clara's mum takes a picture of her poster and puts it up on the town's Facebook page.

Then loads of posters appear in folk's windows.

For weeks, it goes on. The local paper does a story on it: 'THE BE KIND TOWN'.

Nan says that Granda would have loved it, to see the town come together like that.

Alice   In Primary Seven, we have to give a talk. It's for seven minutes in front of the whole school at assembly.

People talk about their hobbies, or pop groups, football teams they like and their pets and stuff but I am going to do mine on runners.

Great runners. Great women runners.

I am going to put up all their names on a PowerPoint with their photos . . .

Jade   . . . Then one week at assembly, Alice from the other Primary Seven class does her talk on great women runners. She had all these photos, she told us about

Alice (*reading under and between* **Jade** – *above*)   . . . 'Kathrine Switzer, Sarah Attar, Wilma Rudoph, Evelyn Ashford, Allyson Michelle Felix, Ellie Greenwood, Merlene Ottey, Kelly Holmes, Angela Mudge, Jo Pavey, Paula Radcliffe, Shelly-Ann Fraser-Pryce.'

Jade   . . . how fast they ran, and what they had to overcome to become these great athletes, and then Hailey carried on telling us about all these other amazing sportswomen. They said that people thought they were not as good as men and they proved them wrong.

Alice (*reading under and between* **Jade** – *above*)   . . . 'Serena and Venus Williams, Megan Rapinoe, Jessica Ennis-Hill, Tanni Grey-Thompson, Nicola Adams, Veronica Ivy, Louise Aitken-Walker, Ellie Simmonds' –

Jade   . . . Alice and Hailey said that knowing about these women inspired them and they hoped to show those who thought girls couldn't be good at sports how wrong they were. Mrs Lomax, our head teacher, said after that . . .

'People's stories can change the world.' Change the world?

Well, that got me and Leila thinking.

Alice   Mum got us t-shirts for our talk with the word 'Champion' written on it, and Dad started singing this song every time Hailey came over to work on our talk.

Alice *starts singing 'We are the Champions'.*

Jade   I was going to do my talk about *Minecraft*, but I decided to do it about my great-nana because . . . Because when we were learning about the Second World War, Jack told us all about his great-grandad – he was a fighter pilot – and Miss told us he was part of the 'Great Generation' and that it was very important for us to remember him, and what

he did for us all . . . My great-nana was part of the great
generation too . . . but you wouldn't know it – like nobody
tells us about great-nana . . . I mean not her exactly, but
about all the people like her . . . Leila tells me about her
great-grandad who was in the British Indian Army, he
fought against the Nazis in Africa . . . She says that we are all
part of the same bit of history . . . But you wouldn't know it
. . .

So just like Alice and Hailey we share our time.

Leila's mum prints out these huge photos of her great-
grandad and my great-nana in their uniforms.

After our talk, we ask Mrs Lomax if the school could include
stories about people like my great-nana and Leila's great-
grandad . . . That it shouldn't just be Jack's grandad that
gets remembered, I say. We are part of the story too, Leila
says, and then we tell her about what happened to us cycling
home, and the graffiti, that it feels connected to that
somehow . . . 'Of being written out of the story', Leila says
. . .

Mrs Lomax takes a while to respond . . . We stand in her
office feeling a bit awkward . . . She asks us to wait a moment
and then leaves us there . . . When she comes back she has
two cups of hot chocolate . . . She says . . .

'Thank you, girls, I learnt something today.'

I mean that was pretty amazing. We taught her something
. . . Our teacher!

Then she asks us if we would like to make a display in the
school corridor, outside the library. A display using our
great-grandparents' photos, and that she will help us to find
more stories about people like our grandparents . . . About
'their contribution' to our country, she says. She will make
sure all the teachers and every class see our wall . . . And I
think . . . Is *this* what we wanted?

Chloe   Mrs Jenkins' granddaughter Jade has no problem with her voice, she is amazing. Really amazing. She did this talk about her great-nana, Mrs Jenkins' mother, at assembly, and then they made this whole display about it for school.

Jade   We spend the next two weeks of lunchtimes working with Mrs Lomax in her room, working on our display, researching all the people from all over the world that came to help – 'Our friends from the Empire' is what Mrs Lomax says . . .

She makes us juice in proper glasses and my nan makes me a special ginger cake to share.

We spend a long afternoon, standing by our wall, as each class comes and takes a look.

It is a bit embarrassing, but Leila says she feels really proud of us. 'We did it', she says. And we did, but honestly, I'm a wee bit annoyed to be missing our maths test, that we'll have to catch up over our library time . . . But Leila tells me that I look like my great-nana, especially when I smile . . . I like that . . . And I smile all afternoon, even when it starts to hurt . . .

We get lots of photos of us by the display, and Mrs Lomax puts it in the newsletter, Nan frames it and hangs it up on her photo wall . . . Right beside great-nana . . . Right beside Granda.

Chloe   Mrs Jenkins tells me that someone tried to destroy Jade's and Leila's –

Jade   – Then one day our display gets drawn on, in big red marker. Blood red. Stop sign red. Red for danger . . . Permanent marker scrawled all over my great-nana's beautiful face.

Chloe   'We should do something', I said to Mrs Jenkins.

Jade   I cried in the middle of the corridor when I saw it. I just burst into this flood of tears. In front of everyone . . . It was horrible . . .

Chloe   'Yes, we should', she replied

Jade   – Mrs Lomax said she was so sorry. 'Oh girls, I am so devastated', she says. She will fix it, she says, and she does . . . but I don't know . . . It still feels broken . . . It all feels broken.

Chloe   Dad would make me feel better about this, he would, but I only get to talk to him on the phone . . . I am not good on the phone –

Jade   – I think Dad is more upset by what happened than me and I am really upset . . . I'm really upset.

Chloe   I miss walking in the woods with him . . . I miss my dad –

Jade   Mum says he can't just ignore stuff like this . . . 'Not anymore' . . .

Chloe   I am going to visit him in Belfast for Easter. He has a new wife now. I am going to be a big sister. I am excited about that, I suppose . . . But I hope the baby is not a girl. Daddy always says I'm his favourite girl. I feel bad thinking that way. I feel bad thinking that he will make his new little girl a hide and teach her the names of all the birds. I feel bad.

Jade   'Not anymore?' . . . What does that even mean?

Chloe   My brother says he doesn't want to come to stupid Belfast, but I think he should. Dad always makes him happy. I am sure he wouldn't be so sad if Dad was here.

Alice   Dad says I was always running up and down the flat. I was 'worse than a puppy', he said, 'always wanting out' . . . Always wanting out.

Scene Two: Chickens

Chloe   The school have six chickens. I help out on Wednesdays and Fridays. I put out the feed, and collect the eggs. Mr Jenkins used to help out too but he died last autumn.

Mr Jenkins' wife comes now but she is not as good with the chickens as Mr Jenkins. She is a bit scared of them. So she sits outside the enclosure and talks to me.

She tells me what a great job I am doing. Sometimes she brings ginger cake.

She likes my drawings. She asked if I would draw her one of the chickens.

So I gave her one I did of Mr Jenkins with Betty the chicken. Betty is the boss chicken. Mr Jenkins called her the grand old lady.

Mrs Jenkins said the picture was just precious.

'Just precious.'

Alice   – My gran is always taking stands. She is always off on marches, for climate change, for peace. Sending letters to her MP asking for help for people. Holding meetings in her front room to talk about how to make things better.

'I am a radical', she says. Champion radical.

Chloe   I worry that it will be too late to save anything if I wait until I am grown up.

Alice   When Mum left home, Gran went to live in Greenham Common. Which was a place where loads of women camped outside an army base to stop the use of nuclear weapons or something . . . Gran said that camp was full of grannies like her.

Chloe   Greta Thunberg is a teenager and is sad like my brother, but she is sad about what is happening to the planet and not about her dad moving to Belfast.

Her dad didn't move to Belfast.

The planet is really sick. Really sick. And we are not doing enough to make it better. Greta is a bit like me and my litter picker, she wants to help, but she is much better at getting attention.

She asked kids to go on strike from school, from all over the world. We were told that we couldn't but I told Mrs Lomax, she is our headteacher, that I knew I would get into trouble but that I couldn't let Greta be like the robin.

I am not sure she got what I meant.

But when I told her I was going to go on strike, even if it was only me, she understood then.

It turned out it was only me in our town that went on strike. And cause I am not that great with people, it was just me not going to school and sitting in my hide all day.

'Not very effective' is what Mum said.

Mrs Lomax asks to see me, asks me what we should do instead. I spend a week thinking in my hide. Write a list of three things for her on a white card. Purple pens.

Meat-free school dinners.

Everyone should walk or cycle to school.

Weekly litter picks in the woods.

Mrs Lomax says, 'Now, Chloe, some of these things will need some planning and thinking about, but it is a good start.'

A good start?

Feels too late for a start of anything . . .

It's far too late for a good start, I think I say, but she is back on her computer and I realise that I am to leave.

'Thank you, Mrs Lomax', I say . . . And leave.

Since then, she has made Wednesdays our 'Care for Our Planet Day', and we are encouraged to walk or cycle to school (if we can).

The other things on my list, we will get to, she says. I am not sure that is enough. It does not feel like enough. It can't just be on Wednesdays that we care.

Alice   'It's what grannies do', she says.

Making the world better is her job, she says. Champion Granny.

Act Four

The Protest

The girls climb.

Chloe   I am with the chickens on one of the 'Care for the Planet' days and Mrs Jenkins asks me why I look so down. I tell her that we need to do something more.

'So how will you get people to change?' she asks. 'I can't change anything', I tell her.

'You got a whole school to walk to school one day a week, it might not be enough, but it's not nothing', she says.

'But most of them already walked to school', I say.

'But now they are walking to school to save the planet', she says. 'Maybe the problem is, they don't know what you know.'

'What do I know?'

'How beautiful and special this town is', she says.

'But it's not just this town, it's the whole world!' I almost scream it. I don't. I don't scream it . . .

'Yes', she says back, 'but it is also this town, Chloe. You need to show people that. Saving this town, that is something people will understand. Small changes can become big changes.'

Small changes can become big changes. I think about that a lot . . . It makes me feel . . . Hopeful, I think.

Jade   Be kind.

Chloe   These signs started appearing all around our town, 'Be Kind'. We became 'The Be Kind Town'. It was strange, like as soon as we said it, it sort of became true.

Alice   Be kind.

Chloe   Mum said that the Facebook page for our town is now full of people saying nice things about other people in the town and thanking people for kind things they have done, rather than complaining. It's refreshing, she said.

Refreshing?

Like a breath of fresh air.

I don't just draw in my notebooks. I like to draw on stones, in paints and chalk. I draw flowers and rainbows on stones I find, and leave them around our garden. It makes Mum happy to find them.

After Dad left, Mum cried all the time and I started to leave stones for her to find with 'I Love You' on them, or 'You Are the Best Mum', because she is, and I love her so much even if Dad doesn't anymore.

After the 'Be Kind' posters, I made stones with 'Be Kind' painted on them and left them in the woods. I put one in the chicken coop too . . . For Betty.

After my chat with Mrs Jenkins, I started to paint my list on stones. Started to leave them all around town. One side – 'Love Our Town'. On the other – 'Eat Local' or 'Walk, Don't Drive' or 'Pick Up Litter' or 'Reuse, Recycle'.

Then I remembered my chalk, and one day I found myself out early, drawing in chalk on the path to school. 'Care for Our Planet', 'Walk to School', 'Meat-Free Wednesdays', 'Litter Pick', and then the next week a drawing of Mr Robin in his backpack saying, I walk to school.

Then Henry the Seagull, with a rubbish bag in his beak and pick up your litter written underneath.

The newspaper took pictures. 'Be Kind Town Says Be Kind to the Planet' was the headline. 'You found your voice', says Mrs Jenkins. 'Not my voice, my chalk', I reply.

I am in the woods. It is early. The sun is making these big shafts of light. Like magic. Like its casting spells. I am there with my bin bag and my litter picker but I am standing very still because there is this beautiful chaffinch on this deep green tree. I am thinking about what colour of pencils I have, or if it would be better in watercolours, and how I don't think I could paint this, it is just too . . .

'Hello?'

And standing there in the path is this old woman in running gear. It's Alice's gran. She has a big black rubbish bag.

'What do you need me to do then?' she says.

'Sorry?' I say.

'I saw your stone about litter picking in the woods. So here I am', she says.

'Oh?' I say.

And I walk to the special place. I am not sure if I speak, sometimes I don't, but she follows me like I have done. And she is not happy when she sees the mess that has been left.

'Right, let's get this sorted', she says.

And then she does, she just gets on and picks stuff up and we clear away all the mess.

At some point I must have told her about Jade and the display, and the boys shouting at Jade and Leila, and about the graffiti I saw on the bridge before Jade's dad painted it away, and about the planet and how sick it is, and how I want to be like Beatrix Potter, and about my dad and the hide, and Mr Jenkins, and the chickens, and about my stones, and my list, and through all of this, she just sits on this big log in the special place and listens, as still as the deer, or the robin. She smiles when I come to a stop.

'Okay, let me help' . . .

She tells me that sometimes you just have to stand up for what you believe in, and for others too, sometimes you have to say enough is enough.

'We need to make a stand', she says.

'Stand up?'

'Why not?' she says.

'Why don't we all just stand up?'

'. . . You mean all together?' I say.

My brother finds me on my knees on the pavement, writing in chalk. I feel him standing there before he speaks. I tell him what I am planning with Lily, that's the lady's name. He says okay, and just walks on.

When I get home, I find him and Mum in the kitchen. Painting stones. For me. They are painting stones for me. And on all the pavements, on posters in windows, on our town's Facebook, on stones is written:

'Stand Up for a Better World Saturday, 10 a.m., Hill Park.'

Lily says she is coming with her friends. My mum is coming, and even my brother says he will be there.

Mrs Jenkins says she will bring cake. Mrs Lomax will bring the school's microphone. My dad rings and says to send him lots of photos.

He says he is so proud of me.

'I love you', he says.

'I love you so much.'

Act Five

Hopeful Town

Alice Gran has made us placards. One for each of us. Mine says, 'I am a girl, hear me roar'. I like that, and Hailey and I roar like lions.

She roars.

There are loads of kids from our year. Even Rory is here. Jade's nan has the school microphone and Mrs Lomax is helping her set it up. We all laugh when it does this big screech of feedback. Gran goes over to help. I watch them laughing. These three women.

Chloe My mum is holding my hand. She squeezes it tight as the park starts to fill up. I can tell she was worried nobody would come. But I have already counted one hundred and it's only 9.30. It will become two hundred by 10. I know it's not anywhere near the whole town but, as Lily says, ten is more than one and two hundred is way more than just me.

My brother comes in just before it starts. He is with his friends. He is waving his rainbow flag and has glitter on his face. He looks so happy. My beautiful boy, Mum whispers, and I look up to see her crying.

She says, it's all good tears. I squeeze her hand. Wave at my brother.

Jade My nan is up there at the mic. 'Funny to see her without Granda', I say. Dad says, 'Oh, he's here.' Then Nan begins to speak with this power in her voice. She asks us all to sit. And everyone does. There are loads and loads of folk here. She counts down from ten. And then at zero she says:

'Stand up for the planet, for our town.'

Then Alice's gran continues . . .

'Stand up for each other, for fairness, for kindness' –

Alice   – and everyone stands and cheers, some folk are
crying and some people are holding hands. Then Mrs
Lomax plays her guitar and starts to sing and all the adults
join in . . .

Then it's over.

People start to leave. The park begins to empty.

We see Chloe starting to pick up litter with her litter picker
and we go over to help her.

Jade   As Nan is packing stuff away, a man comes up to her.
Angry. Red faced.

'I have called the police', he says.

Hailey, Alice and Leila are laughing and helping Alice pick
up the few wee bits that folk have left behind, so my Nan
speaks quietly to him.

'Speak up!'

She asks him what the problem is.

He shouts now. Full voice. Spitting at her.

'You can't just do this. I was here in the park with my kids. I
don't want them exposed to all this, to all youse' –

– 'To what? . . . To whom?' she stops him.

'You know what I am talking about.' Moving closer to her.

'I don't know. Do *you*?' she says.

'All this "Be kind" rubbish, it's nonsense – it's not how the
world works, it's not how people work – you got it?'

'I don't think I do', she says and starts to turn away from
him.

'Well, I've called the police. You know not everyone agrees
with this.'

'With what?'

And he looks like he's about to explode, but then he hisses . . .

'You need permission',

Like a deflating balloon . . . My dad is walking over now.

So Nan says . . . 'Okay' to this man.

This one angry man . . . And we were hundreds.

Chloe   We were hundreds.

Jade   'See you next time', she shouts back.

'Next time?' he splutters.

'Hope to see you there' . . . She smiles at him.

And then she joins us.

Alice   Her hopeful girls.

Chloe   Her hopeful town.

'You know?'

She tells me later.

Jade   'Hope is a superpower. It's yours and the best thing is you can give it away and not lose it. In fact the more you give it away, the more you have.'

The more hope you will have . . .

Then a building roar of voices, of girls, saying 'Here is a girl', ending with a crescendo of 'Here is a girl' and the words 'Here is a girl' shining in the now dark stage. The lights then rise up on the three standing together, holding placards.

The End.

Printed in the USA
CPSIA information can be obtained
at www.ICGtesting.com
LVHW020948171024
794056LV00003B/1012